edZOOcation™ presents
All You Need to Know About
TIGERS

Dear Reader,

We're so glad you're reading our book. Like you, we love animals and are fascinated by the millions of creatures that share our planet. We hope you learn some amazing new facts that help you love them even more.

We also hope you'll feel inspired to take action to protect the animals you learn about. Maybe one day you will even work for one of the zoos or conservations we support!

However you choose to be there for the creatures we all care so much about, we want to be there for you every step of the way. Reach out to us and let us know what you love about animals, what you want to learn about them, and how you want to help them. We can't wait to hear from you!

Sincerely,

Jenny Curtis, Founder

edZOOcation.com

Welcome to the World of Tigers

Tigers are one of the most majestic and powerful animals in the wild. They are the largest of all big cats, with beautiful orange fur and black stripes that make each tiger unique.

FUN FACT!

Tigers can leap up to 33 feet in a single bound!

In this book, you'll discover amazing facts about tigers, their habitats, what they eat, and how we can help protect them.

The Many Faces of Tigers

Tigers come in six subspecies: Bengal, Indochinese, Malayan, Siberian, South China, and Sumatran. Each subspecies has its own unique traits and habitats. For example, the Bengal tiger is the most common, while the Sumatran tiger is the smallest and critically endangered.

The Siberian tiger is the largest subspecies, adapted to live in cold climates.

The Sumatran tiger has the most distinct black stripes.

The Bengal tiger is the most numerous of all tiger subspecies.

Taxonomy

Kingdom: Animalia
(An-i-MALE-yuh) All animals on earth are in this kingdom.
Animalia: Living creature.

Phylum: Chordata
(Kor-daa-tuh) Animals with a spinal cord are grouped in this phylum.
Chordata: Having a spinal cord.

Class: Mammalia
(Ma-MALE-yuh) This level separates mammals, who give birth to live young and make milk, from other vertebrates.
Mammalia: Mamma.

Order: Carnivora
(Car-NIV-er-uh) This order includes animals that primarily eat meat.
Carnivora: Meat-eaters

Family: Felidae
(FEE-li-day) This family includes all cats, from domestic cats to big cats like lions and tigers.
Felidae: Cats.

Genus: *Panthera*
(Pan-THEH-ruh) This genus includes the big cats that can roar, like tigers, lions, leopards, and jaguars.
Panthera: Big cats that can roar.

Species: *Panthera tigris*
(Pan-THEH-ruh TIGH-gris) The scientific name for the tiger.
Panthera tigris: Tigers.

Swimming Tigers

Tigers are excellent swimmers and will often cool off in lakes, rivers, or ponds when the weather gets hot. Not only do they enjoy taking a dip, but they are also strong swimmers, capable of crossing rivers and swimming long distances.

FUN FACT!
A tiger's roar can be heard up to 2 miles away!

UNIQUE
No two tigers have the same stripe pattern.

SPIKY TONGUES
A tiger's tongue is covered with tiny, sharp barbs that help strip meat off bones.

DID YOU KNOW?
Tigers can eat up to 88 pounds of meat in one meal.

11

Tiger Habitats

Tigers live in a variety of habitats, including dense jungles, mangrove swamps, grasslands, and even snowy forests. They are found in parts of Asia, from India and China to Siberia. Each type of habitat provides the tiger with the food and shelter it needs to survive.

Guardians of the Jungle

As apex predators, tigers help maintain a healthy balance in their ecosystems. By controlling the population of herbivores like deer and wild boar, tigers ensure that plants and trees aren't overgrazed. This balance helps keep the forest healthy for all creatures.

Built for Hunting

Tigers are built to be powerful hunters. They have strong muscles, sharp claws, and long canine teeth that can grow up to 3 inches long. Their keen sense of hearing and night vision make them excellent predators. A tiger's stripes help it blend into the tall grass, making it easier to sneak up on prey.

Unique Features of Tigers

Tigers are the largest of all big cats, with males weighing up to 660 pounds. They have long tails for balance and large paws with retractable claws that help them catch their prey.

From Cubs to Kings

A female tiger usually gives birth to 2-4 cubs at a time. Tiger cubs are born blind and weigh about 2 pounds. They stay with their mother for about 2 years, learning how to hunt and survive. Once they are strong enough, they leave to find their own territory.

Did You Know?

Tigers can run at speeds of up to 40 miles per hour, but only in short bursts.

Solitary by Nature

Unlike lions, tigers are solitary animals. Males and females only come together to mate. Mothers are very protective of their cubs and will defend them fiercely against any threat.

How Tigers Talk

Tigers communicate in many ways, from roars and growls to facial expressions and scent markings. Roaring is used to warn other tigers to stay away, while gentle chuffing sounds are used between friends. They also leave scent marks on trees to mark their territory.

Did You Know?
Tigers have a special "chuffing" sound they use as a friendly greeting. Chuffing sounds like a short, breathy puff of air, kind of like a quiet sneeze or a soft 'pfft' sound. It's a friendly noise that tigers make, often to greet other tigers or show affection.

Tiger Tracks and Signs

If you were to track a tiger, you'd look for paw prints, claw marks on trees, and even scat (tiger poop)! A tiger's paw print is large and round, about 5 inches wide, with visible claw marks if the tiger is running or climbing.

FUN FACT!

Tiger scat can tell scientists what the tiger has been eating!

Tigers have retractable claws, which means you won't always see claw marks in their tracks.

The Tiger's Menu

Tigers are carnivores, which means they only eat meat. Their diet includes deer, wild boar, and sometimes even water buffalo. Without tigers, prey populations could grow too large and damage the environment.

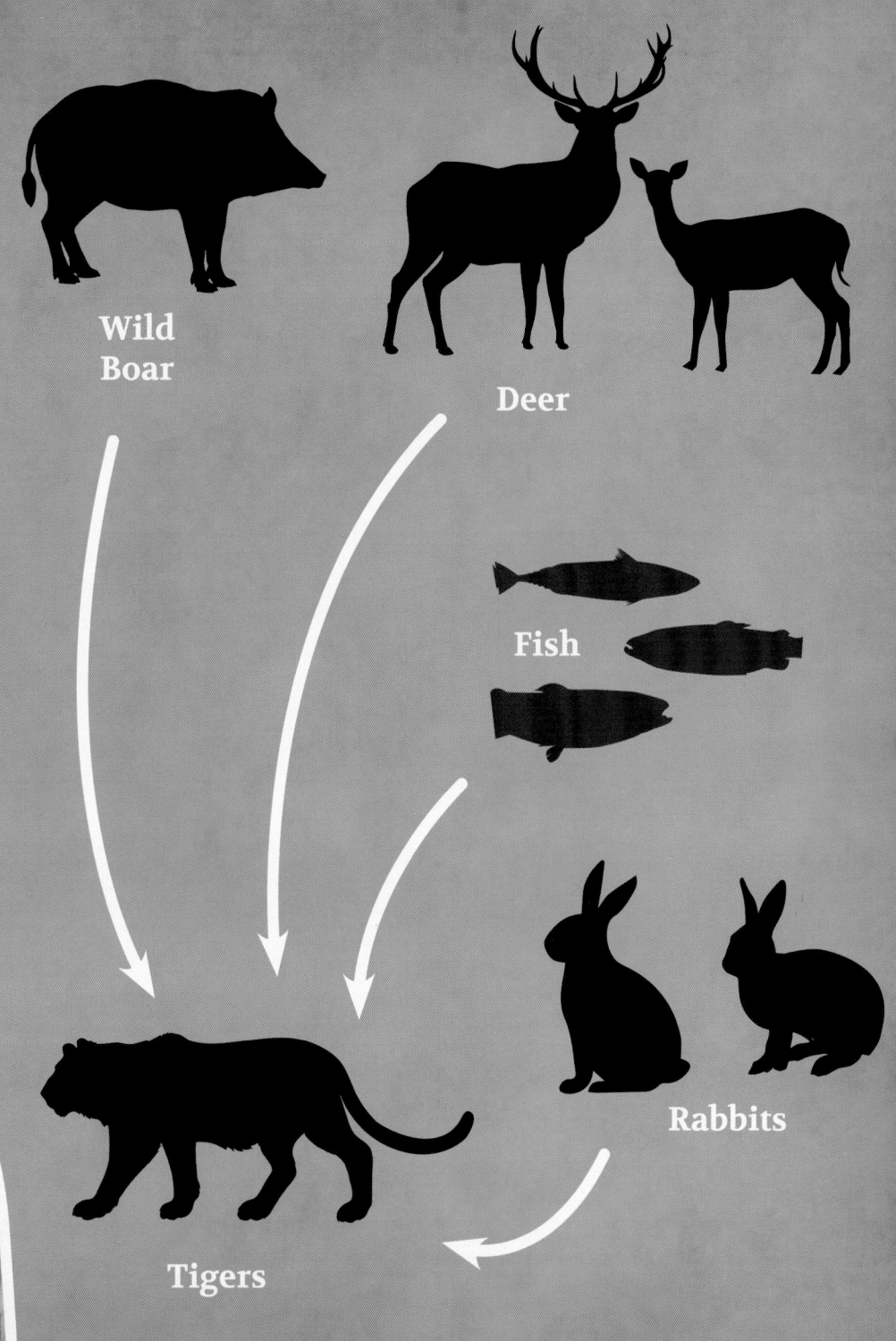

They hunt mostly at night when it's cooler and easier to sneak up on prey.

Tigers mark their territory with scent glands and scratches on trees.

Threats to Tigers

Tigers are endangered due to habitat loss, poaching, and conflict with humans. As forests are cut down for agriculture, tigers lose their homes.

Did You Know?
Tigers have lost over 93% of their historic range.

Some tiger populations, like the Amur tiger in Russia, are slowly increasing thanks to conservation efforts.

Saving the Stripes

Organizations like the WildCats Conservation Alliance are working tirelessly to protect tigers. They focus on anti-poaching efforts, protecting tiger habitats, and educating people about the importance of tigers in the ecosystem. You can help too by supporting these organizations and spreading awareness!

Good News!

Some tiger populations are starting to recover thanks to conservation efforts.

High-Tech Tigers

Did you know that technology is playing a huge role in tiger conservation? Drones, camera traps, and even artificial intelligence are used to track tiger movements and monitor their populations. This helps scientists learn more about tigers and find the best ways to protect them.

Some conservationists use GPS collars to track tiger movements and study their range.

31

Tigers in Culture

Tigers have been a symbol of power and courage in many cultures for thousands of years. They appear in myths, folklore, and even modern media as symbols of strength. In Chinese culture, the tiger is one of the 12 zodiac animals and represents bravery.

FUN FACT!
Tigers are one of the few cats that love water and are strong swimmers.

THE HUNT
Cubs start hunting small animals at around 6 months old.

DID YOU KNOW?
A tiger's tail is about three feet long and helps them keep balance when running and turning.

FOREST CONTROL
Without predators like tigers, some animal populations could grow too large and harm the environment.

How You Can Help

There are many ways you can help tigers, even from your own home. Supporting organizations like the WildCats Conservation Alliance, raising awareness about tiger conservation, and making eco-friendly choices all contribute to the cause. Every small action can make a big difference!

DID YOU KNOW?

Using less paper and recycling can help save the forests where tigers live.

Adopt A Tiger
You can "adopt" a tiger through various conservation programs to help protect them in the wild.

Silly Tigers

Tigers roam both day and night,

Stripes of orange, black, and white.

Through the jungle, wild and free,

Kings and queens of land and tree.

Q: Why did the tiger wear stripes?

A: To avoid being spotted!

Q: How do tigers greet other animals?

A: With a roar!

Q: Why did the tiger cross the road?

A: To prove he wasn't chicken!

Become a
Wildlife Guardian

Everyone can be a Wildlife Guardian by helping our planet. When we help our planet, we help the animals who share it with us, including the powerful and beautiful tigers.

Here are ways you can help tigers:

Reduce, Reuse, Recycle
Help protect tiger habitats by reducing waste and conserving resources. This can help reduce deforestation and pollution in tiger habitats.

Support Sustainable Products
Choose products that are certified as sustainable, especially those that help reduce deforestation. Look for labels like FSC (Forest Stewardship Council) on paper and wood products.

Raise Awareness
Share what you've learned about tigers with friends and family. Awareness is the first step to protecting these incredible animals.

edZOOcation.com

edZOOcation™ Readers
Inspiring Love for Animals Through Reading

Learning about your favorite animal just got even more fun with our edZOOcation Factivity Books. Filled with jaw-dropping facts, amazing photos, and fun games, you'll learn everything you never knew you wanted to know about the wild world of animals.

Become an expert in a new animal every month with an edZOOcation subscription.

ISBN 978-1-965081-07-5
US $9.99